Everyday NFC
Near Field Communication Explained

Second Edition

Hsuan-hua Chang

For Michelle,
Happy transition!
Hsuan-hua Chang   Nov 2014

ISBN: 0982434022
ISBN-13: 978-0982434024

CONTENTS

FIGURES

ACKNOWLEDGMENTS

My appreciation goes to my family who supports me in learning and living my life fully, and to my friends who believe in me and are always there for me.

David Williams and Julie Chang Schulman are my editors. I thank them for their patience and wisdom. Additional thanks to David Schulman, Linda Schulman, Jean Marie Hung, Karl Weaver, Ranjan Kumar Naidu, and Tung-Yuen Lau for their review and feedback.

Special thanks to:

Koichi Tagawa for providing information on NFC Forum

Masayuki Takezawa for providing information on Sony products

Randy Vanderhoof for providing information on Smart Card Alliance

Kevin Gillick for information on GlobalPlatform

Poken, ScholarChip, TapWise, Taganize and Tapit for providing information on tag management platforms.

About This Book

Albert Einstein once said, "If you can't explain it simply, you don't understand it well enough." Since I understand Near Field Communication (NFC) well, my intention in writing this book is to explain NFC technology in such a way that my readers can take advantage of its exciting potential.

NFC is an innovative technology that has yet to be widely adopted. However, when consumers and businesses fully understand and adopt this technology, NFC will transform not only the consumer experience, but also our everyday lives. For example, 3800 athletes from 204 countries were able to follow events, engage in activities, retrieve and store information, and get to know other participants in the Young Olympic Games at Nanjing, China in August 2014 using Yogger, an NFC-enabled wearable device.

New business opportunity will reward early adopters for their vision and foresight. The potential for transformation brought by NFC technology inspires me. Therefore, I am updating my readers with the latest developments.

Updates:

This is the second edition of "Everyday NFC". It includes new information on tag management, mobile payment, Host Card Emulation (HCE), use cases and the Apple Pay mobile wallet available via iPhone6.

Book Structure:

This book is organized into five chapters:

- **What is NFC**
  A technology overview with examples and summaries.
- **Where is NFC Now**
  Examples of current use cases that demonstrate recent NFC applications in mobile payment, banking, gaming, transit, health care and many more.
- **How to Use NFC**
  Brief summaries that describe the use of NFC phones/tags/wallet and a technology overview of the two communication modes, three operating modes, NFC secure transactions and HCE.
- **Who are the NFC Players**
  Summary of the NFC ecosystem and various industry standard groups.
- **Why Use NFC**
  Summary of the value of NFC and a comparison with other wireless technologies.

Who Should Read This Book?

This book is written for people who are interested in learning about NFC and want to explore the possibility of this technology. This includes application (app) developers, business executives, entrepreneurs, innovators and consumers who are eager to adopt new technology.

It is also useful for executives who are responsible for making decisions about NFC projects.

For a brief general overview of the technology, see the introduction section of each chapter.

Supplemental Reading

Go to everydaynfc.com to see the most recent news and discussions.

Go to EverydayNFC in Paper.li to read the daily news about the NFC technology.

Chapter 1: What is NFC?

Introduction

Near Field Communication (NFC) is a contactless technology using Radio Frequency, eliminating the need for physical contact. When NFC is integrated into wireless devices, it serves as another option for wireless connectivity; other similar technologies are WIFI and Bluetooth.

With NFC, mobile devices can easily connect within four centimeters of each other to retrieve and exchange data (Figure 1). It operates at 13.56 MHz and transfers data at up to 424 Kbit/second.

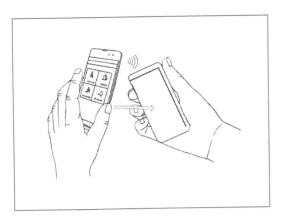

Figure 1: Two NFC-enabled phones exchange data

At the same time, NFC is not just a connectivity technology; it is also an enabling technology. For example, NFC can enable mobile payment and secure access to buildings or public transportation.

NFC can also initiate many automated processes with NFC tags (Figure 2).

Figure 2: An NFC-enabled phone reads data from an NFC tag

The following are two examples of NFC in action:

1.   ORCA Cards

Have you ever ridden a bus in Seattle? In the greater Seattle area, the ORCA card system was launched in 2009 to consolidate payment options for the different branches of mass transit. Riders who carry an ORCA card can get on a King County Metro or Sound Transit bus, Light Rail train or even a ferry without needing cash for the fare. When the ORCA card is swiped across a card reader, the fare is deducted from the card's account value (Figure 3), called an "e-purse" (King County, n.d.).

Figure 3: An ORCA reader reads an ORCA card

Technical summary:

- The ORCA card is a "smart card" with NFC technology.
- A microchip named MIFARE DESfire is embedded inside the ORCA card (Raschke, 2011).
- Information is stored in the microchip, which has a secured microcontroller and internal memory.
- An antenna is embedded in the ORCA card to enable tracking of the card and data transmission.
- When an ORCA card is placed within 4 cm of the card reader, the card reader transfers energy to the microchip in the ORCA card.
  - Wireless communication is established between the ORCA card and the card reader.
  - The data transfer is completed.
  - The ORCA payment process is completed.

2. Assa Abloy's Digital Key Service

When a guest checks in at <u>Hotel Porta Fira Santos</u> in France, the service provider (Assa Abloy) is able to transfer room key information to a SIM card in any NFC-enabled phone (Figure 4).

The guest can then access the hotel room by tapping their mobile phone to the lock of the room. This example was demonstrated at the GSMA Mobile World Congress (ABLOY, 2013).

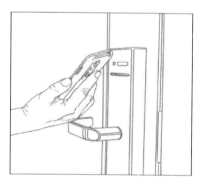

Figure 4: An NFC phone unlocks a door

Technical summary:

- A guest checks in at the hotel.
- The hotel room number is sent to a back-end platform (Assa Abloy) with the guest's information.
- The platform transfers the hotel room number and key over the air to a smart card residing in the quest's mobile phone.
- When the mobile phone is placed within 4 cm of the lock,
  - The wireless communication is established between the phone and the lock.
  - The data transfer is completed between the lock reader and the smartcard in the phone.
  - The room is then unlocked.

Technical Overview

This section provides a technical overview about NFC Data Exchange Format, NFC devices and NFC tags. Understanding these details can help expand knowledge and provide important background information for the available applications of NFC in business.

NFC Data Exchange Format (NDEF)

When we tap an NFC-enabled phone to another NFC phone or an NFC tag, data is exchanged in NDEF format that is the standard of the NFC Forum.

The NDEF format consists of NDEF Messages and NDEF Records. An NDEF Message is an array of NDEF Records with a header and payload (Figure 5). If the payload is large, then the records can be chained to support bigger data. It depends on the application and tag type to determine exactly how many NDEF Records can be encapsulated in an NDEF Message.

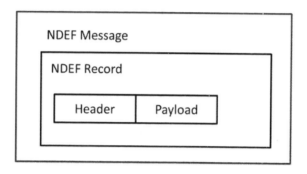

Figure 5: NDEF Message format

Record Type Definition (RTD) specifies rules for building a standard NDEF Record type. There are four RTDs: Text, URI, Smart Poster, and Signature. For detailed information about NDEF data structure format, please refer to <u>NDEF technical specification</u> (Forums, 2006).

NFC Devices

ABI Research estimated that 500 million NFC devices will be shipped in 2014 and HIS forecasted that 1.2 billion NFC units will be shipped in 2018 (Figure 6). NFC is truly becoming integral to the mobile device.

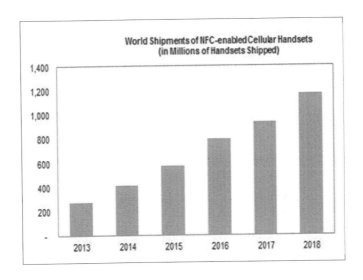

Figure 6: World Shipments of NFC-enabled handsets
millions of handsets shipped) Source: HIS Inc.
February 2014

- Mobile Phones, Tablets and Laptops

  Feature (non-smart) phones are not NFC-enabled because
  they do not contain NFC components. Many smartphones
  are NFC-enabled. A list of NFC-enabled phones can be
  found at the website of NFC World, i.e.
  www.nfcworld.com.

  An NFC-enabled device can also be read by an NFC
  reader to perform a mobile payment (Figure 7).

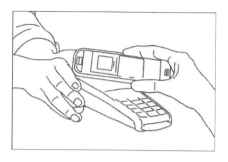

Figure 7: An NFC-enabled phone taps a reader to perform payment

NFC-enabled tablets are a new market segment. More than two dozen brands of NFC-enabled tablets were released from 2012 to 2014. For example, The Hisense Sero 7 Pro is a low cost (under $100) Android tablet released in May 2014. The Dell Venue 11 Pro is a Windows 8.1 tablet PC released in April 2014. A list of NFC-enabled tablets can be found at the website of NFC World, i.e. www.nfcworld.com.

- Other Devices

  Other NFC-enabled devices are also arriving on the market. For example, Tap2Tag introduced NFC wristbands in June 2014 to retrieve a person's medical history (Boden, Tap2Tag launches NFC medical alert devices, 2014). Other wearable devices such as rings can unlock phones, pass on digital business cards, start cars or unlock doors (McGregor, 2013).

In January 2014, Canon introduced three compact cameras (ELPH 340 HS, N100, SX600 HS) that are NFC-enabled so that they can send photos to and from Android devices with a tap.

Plus Prevention released a range of medical devices. All data from these devices can be transferred by a simple tap to any Android NFC smartphone (Clark S. , 2013) (Figure 8).

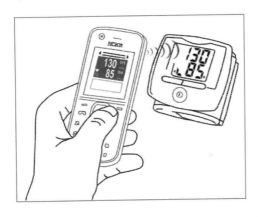

Figure 8: An NFC-enabled phone taps a medical device

ABI Research believes that from 2014 onwards, computing products, peripherals and automotive will have greater adoption of NFC, and consequently, smartphones will decline from a peak of 80% of all NFC device shipments in 2013 to less than 60% in 2017 (Newswire, 2013)

NFC Tags

NFC tags (Figure 9) are passive devices used to communicate with active NFC devices. At the heart of every NFC tag is an NFC chip. It contains a small memory storage chip and a radio chip attached to an antenna. It does not have a power source and can be powered up by an NFC device through a magnetic field (XDA, 2013).

Figure 9: An NFC tag

The price for a blank tag ranges from US $0.70 to $1.25 based on the memory and features. Encoding costs range from about US $ 0.05 to 0.25 per tag based on the content and security requirements.

Using an NFC-enabled Android device, you can write to a NFC tag and make it "read only". Once a tag is encoded to read-only, it can't be provisioned again. This is referred to as a "write protected" tag.

Windows devices cannot format a tag as "read only". This is one major drawback, since tag content formatted on a Windows device can be changed.

NFC tags can be programmed and embedded in business cards, smart posters, stickers, wrist bands and promotional materials (Figure 10). They are extremely useful in the distribution of information and the promotion of products and services. They can also launch tasks, preform configurations and initiate apps when being tapped by an NFC-enabled device.

Figure 10: A user taps his NFC phone on the tag of a poster

Tag Types:

The NFC Forum released the NFC tag specification in 2007 for four types of tags. The newest updates of the specifications were published in 2014.

- Type 1:

    - Products examples: Broadcom BCM20203, Innovision Topaz
    - Standards: ISO/IEC-14443A
    - Transfer Speed: 106 Kbps
    - Read or re-write capable; can be configured to read-only
    - Memory availability: 96 bytes and expandable to 2kbyte

- Type 2:

    - Products examples: NXP Mifare Ultralight, NXP Mifare Ultralight C and NTAG21x (with built-in security features)
    - Standards: ISO/IEC-14443A
    - Transfer Speed : 106 Kbps
    - Read and re-write capable; can be configured to read-only
    - Memory availability : 48 bytes and expandable to 2kbytes

- Type 3:

  o Products examples: Sony FeliCa
  o Standards: JIS X 6319-4 (Japanese standard FeliCa)
  o Transfer Speed : 212 or 424 Kbps
  o Read and re-writable, or read-only (pre-configured at manufacture)
  o Memory availability: variable, theoretical limit is 1Mbyte per service

- Type 4:

  o Products examples: NXP DESFire, NXP SmartMX-JCOP, Calypso B
  o Standards: Compatible with ISO/IEC 14443 (A&B)
  o Transfer Speed : 106 Kbps, 212 and 424 Kbps
  o Read, re-writable, or read-only.
  o The memory availability: variable, up to 32Kbytes per service

Tag Management:

There are quite a few vendors providing NFC tag management platforms that enable users to encode and manage NFC tags.

Poken (www.poken.com) has a global reputation for enhancing events and conferences, especially in the fields of Travel, IT, Finance and Medicine.

ScholarChip (www.scholarchip.com) offers an education

management platform for NFC tags placed on loaned school items such as laptops, tablets, class equipment and anything else that needs to be tracked and returned.

TapWise (www.tapwise.com) provides nTags as well as a broad suite of management tools including remote reprogramming and real-time user engagement analytics.

Taganize (www.taganize.com) offers a way to re-provision its users' read-only tag. A Taganize tag can also be generated into a QR code.

Some vendors analyze device/tag interactions. For instance, in August 2013 Coca-Cola conducted an NFC marketing campaign in one hundred Australian stores utilizing Tapit (www.tapit.com). The Tapit platform was able to collect a variety of analytic information about participating customers, including the model of handset, operating system, carrier and browser types used. (Boden, NFC World, 2013)

Chapter 2: Where Is NFC Now?

Introduction

MarketsandMarkets estimated that the NFC market will be worth $16.25 billion by 2022 (MarketsandMarkets, 2014). There will be tremendous opportunity in this NFC landscape.

With Apple's NFC-enabled iPhone 6 release and the soon to be released NFC-enabled iWatch, the NFC adoption rate will accelerate through technology awareness. The whole NFC ecosystem will be impacted positively.

Devices and Software Overview

Below is some data to show how devices and software have progressed with NFC.

Devices

The volume of the NFC-enabled devices shipped (Figure 11):

- In 2010, 3 million were shipped.
- In 2011, 30 million were shipped (PhoneArena, 2012).
- In 2012, 125 million were shipped.
- In 2013, 275 Million were shipped (IHS, 2014).

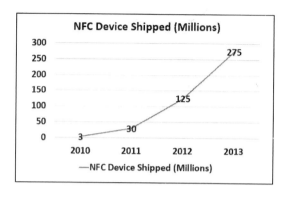

Figure 11: NFC devices shipping stat 2010-2013

Operating System (OS)

The operating system release timeline (Figure 12) as follows:

- In 2006, the first NFC-enabled phone (Nokia 6131) was release by Nokia.

- In 2010, the first Android NFC phone (Nexus S) was released by Google.

- In 2011, Blackberry released two NFC phones (Bold 9900 & 9930).

- In 2012, the first Windows Phone (Lumia 610) with NFC was released by Nokia (Davies, 2012).

- In 2014, Apple released NFC-enabled mobile payment iPhone6 with iOS8.

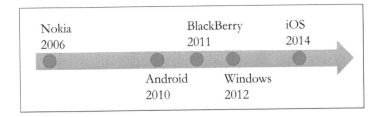

Figure 12: NFC phone release based on OS

Software Framework

The software framework timeline:

- In 2010, open NFC API (reader/writer mode) for Android (Gingerbread) was released through NXP and Trusted Logic (News N. , 2010).
- In 2011, Blackberry released Java SDK v7.0 for both tag reading/writing and card emulation apps (Clark S. , 2011).
- In 2011, Peer to Peer mode became available for Android (Admin, 2011). You can find API documentations and NFC sample codes at Android's <u>NFC Basics page</u>.
- In 2013, Windows 8 was released with <u>proximity APIs</u>.
- In 2014, <u>MIFARE SDK</u> was released, allowing the development of NFC-enabled Android apps.

Use Cases & Current NFC Products and Services Examples

In recent years, early adopters have started focusing on the creation of NFC products and services. NFC applications continue to be released.

Below are examples of applications which demonstrate the versatility of NFC technology.

Mobile Wallet/Payment

A mobile wallet enables you to use your mobile phone for making payments. Your credit card information is entered and saved in your mobile wallet. An NFC mobile wallet is composed of a few components: a mobile application (app), payment options (credit cards), an authentication method for user identification, and NFC for wireless transmission.

- Apple Pay is an NFC mobile wallet app provided by Apple. It is available in October 2014. It works with the iPhone 6, iPhone 6+ and iWatch.

  Apple writes, "There's no need to open an app or even wake your display thanks to the innovative Near Field Communication antenna in iPhone6. To pay, just hold your iPhone near the contactless reader with your finger on Touch ID. You don't even have to look at the screen to know your payment information was successfully sent. A subtle vibration and beep lets you know." (Apple, 2014)

  Passbook is used to store credit card information. One can enter new credit card information manually or use the iSight camera to capture the card information and add it to the iPhone.

The banks participating in the launch include: America Express, Bank of America, Capital One, Chase, Citibank and Wells Fargo.

- Softcard Mobile Wallet (formally ISIS Mobile Wallet, renamed in September 2014) is an NFC mobile payment joint-venture between AT&T, T-Mobile and Verizon. Softcard mobile app was released in November 2013.

  Consumers can enter and store American Express, American Serve, Chase or Wells Fargo credit cards to Softcard mobile wallet.

  Softcard joint venture is actively working with Apple to enable Softcard mobile wallet on the iPhone in 2015 using an integrated secure SIM-based hardware solution.

  Softcard can also provide value-added offer integration for retail vendors; for example, Subway customers who load their rewards card into the Softcard app can tap their phones at the point of sale to pay and receive reward credits (Whitney, 2014) (Sep2014).

Gaming

- Nintendo has been leveraging NFC to enrich the gaming experience of Wii U players. For example, players can now use the NFC interface built into the Game Pad Controller to purchase games with a prepaid e-card.

  Nintendo has also integrated NFC into gaming itself. Amiibo is an NFC-enabled figurine that can gain skills and attributes proportional to user interaction. When a player touches Amiibo to the Game Pad, his character's data is downloaded into the game, and he can also send information back to his character. Therefore, Amiibo's attributes get a small boost in each battle which increases overall level, defense and attack powers in a game. (June 14) (Boden, Nintendo unveils Amiibo NFC figures that work with multiple Wii U and 3DS games, 2014)

  In addition to increasing purchasing and playing power, NFC is also allowing Nintendo users to import photos and content from their phones to their game consoles through a peer to peer data exchange mode (wiiudaily, 2014) (Jun2014).

- McDonald's announced the rollout of Happy Table in Asia. This video shows how NFC tags are utilized to transform a regular table into a gaming platform. This is an example of how NFC can be used with furniture (Aug2013).

Transportation:

- London Metro plans on saving consumers' time and energy by offering news at 10,000 bus stops in the UK via NFC. By using NFC devices to tap tags at any <u>Metro touch point ad Panel</u>, people can connect to the Metro landing page in order to access news. This is an example of using NFC tags to direct consumers to a designated website (Sep2013).

HealthCare

- <u>Tag2Tag</u> stores users' medical information on a secured server and allows NFC-enabled cards, wristbands, and NFC tags to access the information in an emergency situation. (Jun2014) In this case, NFC is used as an access device.

Wearable:

- Apple unveiled iWatch on September 2014. It is an NFC-enabled smartwatch that users can use to make tap payments. It will also use NFC to track and monitor health and fitness data (Sep2014).

- <u>NFC Ring</u> can be used to unlock doors, save information, scan data and perform many other tasks. Inside the ring, there are two NFC chips. One chip is used to transmit data, and the other stores sensitive information. This

YouTube video demonstrates these functionalities. NFC ring is an example of a wearable, contactless device with NFC capability (Aug2013).

Consumer Electronics

- Sony unveiled a family of photographic zoom lenses with integrated image sensors that can be connected to Android or iOS smartphones via NFC and WiFi to provide a high quality, DSLR-like camera experience. This is an example of using NFC to extend the functionality of smartphones (Sep2013).

- By downloading an app into an NFC-enabled phone and tapping the phone onto the Samsung Xpress printer, one can easily print, scan or fax. This video demonstrates this capability of NFC technology. This is an example of NFC pairing (Aug2013).

Insights from Data Collection

- TapWise provided its NFC data collection and analytics platform to Tribeca Film Festival. Promotional posters with HID NFC tags were used to digitally distribute free movie tickets. These smart posters were tapped a total of 8,195 times by 1,156 individual mobile devices (May2013).

- The Coca-Cola Rewards program reported, "More than one-third of active ISIS Mobile Wallet users in Austin have loaded a My Coke Rewards card into their wallet since our pilot began, and 90 percent of these are new to the My Coke Rewards program." This is an example of using NFC mobile payment to boost participation in consumer loyalty programs (Jul2013).

Event / Trade-shows

- Poken supported NFC utilization at the 2014 Youth Olympic Games in Nanjing. Each participant in the event received a Yogger, an NFC-enabled device, which was used to exchange contact and social media information with other participants(Aug2014). (BusinessWire, Nanjing Youth Olympic Village Promotes High-Tech Socializing, 2014)

Food/Drink Quality Control

- Thinfilm introduced NFC smart labels with temperature sensors that can be used for food packaging or tracking wine temperature. Consumers can use an NFC-enabled phone to check whether a product has been kept at its required temperature through the supply chain (May2014).

Marketing

- <u>Crosscliq published</u> Canada's first Blackberry NFC-enabled magazine ad. NFC tags were embedded in the Rogers Connected Magazine. When an ad is tapped by a Blackberry NFC-enabled phone, a holiday gift is offered (Jan2013). This is an example of embedding NFC tags into printed material.

- <u>Tenet Computer Group Inc.</u> released the <u>GreenRack Cloud service</u> that enables people to globally distribute information. Tapping your smartphone to a GreenRack station launches the Information e-Concierge, which automatically scans associated QR codes or NFC tags. This is an example of combining location-based content with on-demand publishing (May2013).

Chapter 3: How to use NFC

Introduction

It is exciting to test NFC functionalities when you obtain an NFC phone. You might want to scan a tag or tap another NFC-enabled phone to exchange data, or you might want to exercise your mobile payment options. This section shows you how.

A special note about the newly released iPhone 6: All other NFC functionalities besides Apply Pay mobile wallet have been disabled by Apple. Therefore, iPhone6 doesn't have full NFC functionality and cannot be used to read or write an NFC tag.

- **To activate NFC functionality on an Android or Windows phone:**
  1. Go to Home.
  2. Go to Applications (or Apps on Android phone only).
  3. Go to Settings.
  4. For Android: check the NFC app
  5. For Windows 8: check the tap+send app.

- **To read an NFC tag:**
  1. Make sure that the NFC functionality is enabled and the screen is active. You do not need to download an app to read or scan an NFC tag.
  2. Place your phone over the tag within 4 cm (Figure 13).
  3. When asked, accept the request to receive the data exchange.

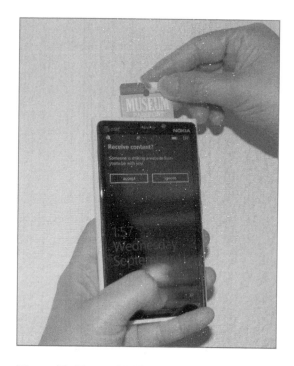

Figure 13: Tap an NFC-enabled phone to read an NFC tag

- **To Write to an NFC Tag using an Android Phone**
  1. Make sure that the NFC functionality is enabled on the device.
  2. Download NXP TagWrite app from Google Play Store.
  3. Click on "Create, write and store" to create a NFC data set.

4. Type in a link to a web page.

5. Tap your phone to an NFC Forum Type 2 Tag when you see the screen display: "Ready to store or share the selected content" as shown (Figure 14).

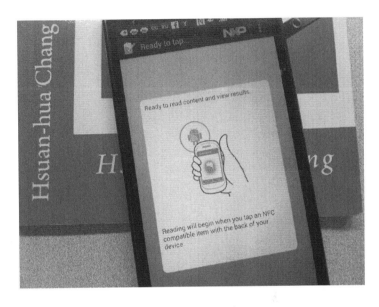

Figure 14: TapWriter app is ready to write content to an NFC Tag

6. See "Store successful" message on the Result window. This confirms that new content has been written to the tag.

- **To Use Google Wallet:**

1. Make sure the mobile device runs on Android 3.2 (Gingerbread) or higher.

2. Enable NFC functionality through Setup.
3. Download Google Wallet app from Google Play Store.
4. If you have not used Google Wallet, you need to:
    1) Set up an account.
    2) Choose a wallet pin.
    3) Add a method of payment.

5. Use the NFC device to pay your bill at stores that have NFC readers.

- **To Use Softcard (formally ISIS) Mobile Wallet on an Android Phone**
  1. Make sure that the NFC functionality is enabled on the device.
  2. Ensure your device is equipped with the required Enhanced NFC SIM card with Secure Element.
  3. Download Softcard Mobile Wallet app from Google Play Store.
  4. Set up an access PIN.
  5. Add the method of payment.
  6. Use the NFC device to pay your bill at stores that have NFC readers.
      1) Open the Softcard Mobile Wallet app and enter your PIN.
      2) Select a payment card to use.
      3) Hold the back of your phone over the contactless symbol on the terminal at checkout.

- **To Use Apple Pay Mobile Wallet on an iPhone6**
  1. If you don't have Passbook setup, add the credit or debit card from your iTunes account to Passbook by simply entering the card security code.
  2. Add a new card, use your iSight camera to instantly capture your card information or simply type it in manually.
  3. The first card you add automatically becomes your default card.
  4. Make sure you have iOS 8.1 (Settings/General/Software Updates shows iOS version)
  5. Use iPhone to pay your bill at stores that have NFC readers
     1) Hold your iPhone near the contactless reader with your finger on Touch ID
     2) Make payment with the default credit card or choose another credit card to pay by selecting a new default in Settings or go to Passbook any time to pay with a different card.

Technology Overview

This section explains the technology behind NFC functionalities. It includes NFC communication modes, NFC operating modes, the secure mode components that ensure the security of mobile transactions and Hosted Card Emulation (HCE). This information will give you additional background for NFC operation and infrastructure.

Two NFC Communication Modes

The two communication modes are active and passive.

- **Active mode**:
  Each NFC-enabled device in communication has a power supply. This mode allows two NFC devices to tap each other for data exchange (Figure 15).

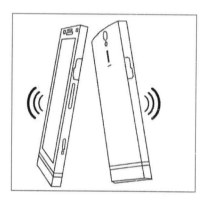

Figure 15: NFC-enabled phones exchange data in active mode

- **Passive mode**:
  The prime NFC-enabled device generates radio signals, and the receiving device is powered by the magnetic field of the prime device. This mode allows a passive NFC tag to be read by an active NFC reader.

  An ORCA Card transaction (Figure 16) is an example of passive mode usage. The ORCA card itself is always in passive mode and does not need a power supply. The ORCA card reader is in active mode. When the ORCA card is placed close to the reader, the reader powers the ORCA card and starts the data exchange.

Figure 16: A passive NFC card is read by an active NFC reader

Three NFC Operating Modes

The three operating modes are Reader/Writer, Peer-to-Peer and Card Emulation.

- **Reader/Writer**: This is an open mode; an NFC-enabled device can read from an NFC tag or write to an NFC tag based on the ISO 14443 standard and FeliCa schemes.

- **Peer-to-Peer**: This is an open mode; two NFC-enabled devices can exchange data based on the ISO 18092 standard, which include two modes; P2P passive and P2P active. An example of this is the exchange of digital business cards (Figure 17). In this case:
  - o After introductions, one party initiates the exchange with an NFC-enabled device and sends a business card to the other party.
  - o The other party, as a target, will send a business card back to the initiator.

  Two NFC standards are used in this case:

  - o Logical Link Control Protocol (LLCP): The NFC Forum has specified this protocol to enhance the Peer-to-Peer mode of operation. LLCP sits on top of the ISO 18092 in the protocol stack and is used to establish communication.
  - o Simple NDEF Exchange Protocol (SNEP): This is an application-level protocol released by the NFC Forum for sending or receiving messages

between two NFC-enabled devices (NFC-Forum, n.d.).

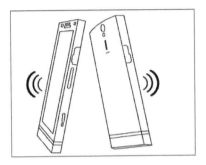

Figure 17: Digital business cards are exchanged when two NFC-enabled phones tap each other

- **Card Emulation**: This is a secure mode; an NFC device is used in passive mode to emulate the behavior of a contactless card based on the ISO 14443 standard. Mobile payment transactions are completed in this mode (Figure 18).

In such a transaction:

o An NFC reader generates a magnetic field through its antenna.
o The reader sends a command to the NFC-enabled phone the same way it would send a command to a contactless smart card.
o The NFC-enabled phone sends its response to the NFC reader.

Figure 18: An example of card emulation

NFC Secure Transaction

An NFC secure transaction supports secured mobile applications such as mobile wallet and building access. A common infrastructure includes Secure Element (SE), Over-the-Air (OTA) download via Trusted Service Manger (TSM) and Trusted Execution Environment (TEE) in some cases. Understanding the secure transaction provides important background for designing or choosing a secured NFC product or service.

- **Secured Element (SE)**

  The Secure Element (SE) is a tamper resistant smart card that includes secure microcontrollers, a CPU, an operating system, memory and a crypto engine. It is used to store sensitive information for NFC products and services. For example, a hotel room access application can store hotel key information on the SE or credential information to authenticate mobile payment.

The current implementation of SE is as follows:

- o Hardware Format:
    - ➢ Fixed: SE in the phone, this is a device manufacturer centric approach. Apple uses this approach.
    - ➢ Removable: UICC/SIM-based SE, this is the telecom operator centric approach. Softcard uses this approach.
    - ➢ Attached: SE in a phone sleeve or tag, this approach is used for Apple devices that don't have NFC capability.

- o Software Format:
    - ➢ Cloud-based: SE is stored in the Cloud. Google Wallet uses this approach.
    - ➢ Not Cloud-based: SE is stored in the phone application.

Mobile phones come with a Universal Integrated Circuit Card (UICC) smart card that has a Subscriber Identification Module (SIM) to identify subscribers.

If subscribers want to make an NFC mobile payment, they need to get a UICC with SE embedded. A UICC/SIM-based SE facilitates NFC Card Emulation Mode for secured payment transactions. As a result, the carrier has control over storage and access of the SE (Figure 19).

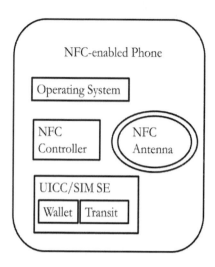

Figure 19: NFC-enabled phone with UICC/SIM SE

SE implementations can be software based. For example, Inside Secure (SE) has a Cloud-based NFC SE solution so that a physical SE in the phone is not needed (Figure 20). When a consumer conducts a transaction, encrypted data will be pulled from the SE in the Cloud (Clark0925, 2012).

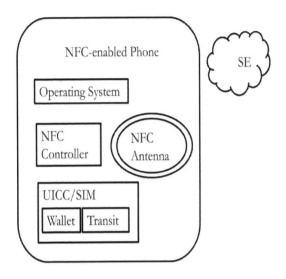

Figure 20: Cloud-based SE

- **Trusted Service Manager (TSM)**

  Storing, accessing and managing information in a SIM-based SE requires an infrastructure that facilitates over-the-air (OTA) download and management of SE. One approach, endorsed by the GSMA, is to deploy TSM. TSM shall be compliant with Global Platform standards and GP messaging specifications (Global Platform, 2013).

  There are two types of TSM as follows:

- o **Mobile Network Operator (MNO) TSM**

  MNO TSM performs management of credentials and OTA provisioning stored in the SIM-based SE that is in the mobile device on behalf of the service provider. It performs distribution, provision and management of the NFC apps in the SE (Figure 21).

  MNO TSM may have the following capabilities:
  - ➤ Interconnection with Mobile Network Operations (MNO) and Service Providers (SP)
  - ➤ MNO management
  - ➤ SP management
  - ➤ SP application management
  - ➤ OTA provisioning and mobile device management
  - ➤ Maintenance of end-to-end security

- o **Service Provider (SP) TSM**

  SP TSM acts as a bridge between service providers and MNO TSM that operate by mobile network operators to enable mobile commerce such as mobile payments (Figure 21).

  SP TSM may have the following capabilities:
  - ➤ Management of multiple MNO and SP interfaces
  - ➤ Management of rule engines and workflow
  - ➤ Management of applets and security domains (SDs) on SE
  - ➤ Lifecycle management of NFC service applications
  - ➤ OTA support

- ➢ OTA card management for all SE implementations
- ➢ Customer service
- ➢ Reporting capabilities
- ➢ Billing support
- ➢ Direct communication with the SE for card management functions without connecting through the MNO TSM

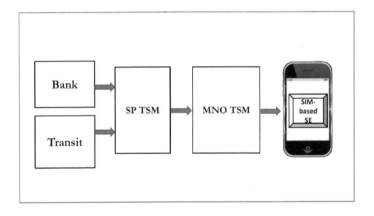

Figure 21: SP TSM and MNO TSM

This approach has been adopted by Softcard Mobile Wallet. It's a telecom operator-centric approach since telecoms own TSMs (the access of the SIM-based SE) and the real estate on the SIM.

- **Trusted Execution Environment (TEE)**

The Global Platform Trusted Execution Environment (TEE) solution is designed for enhancing mobile security, and it also enhances NFC secure mode operations that use UICC/SIM-based SE. The specifications for card, device and systems can be found at www.globalplatform.org/specifications.asp.

The TEE is a secure area that resides in the main processor of a mobile device, and sensitive data may be stored in this trusted environment. It offers end-to-end security for the trusted applications by providing protection, confidentiality, integrity and data access rights. This level of security is sufficient for some applications (Gillick, n.d.).

The TEE offers a trusted user interface for SE. It may also filter access to applications stored on the SE (Figure 22). Use cases are as follows: secure remote access (authentication, encryption and secure display), secure email (authentication, encryption and signing) and secure physical access (authentication and unique protocols) (Cattaneo, 2014).

Industry is adopting TEE gradually. For example, Qualcomm has announced that it plans to integrate TEE with its NFC chip (Balaban, 2013). Apple joined Global Platform in September 2014.

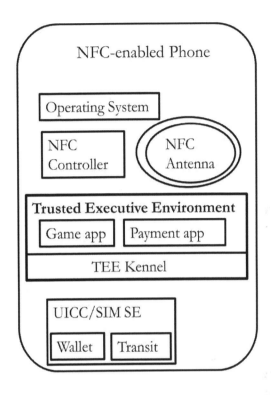

Figure 22: Trusted Execution Environment

Host Card Emulation (HCE)

HCE was a term created by the founders of SimplyTapp, Doug Yeager and Ted Fidelski, in 2011 to describe the ability to transact with remotely operated smart cards.

Many NFC-enabled devices support NFC card emulation. In most cases, the card is emulated by Secure Element (SE). HCE's card emulation allows applications to emulate a card and talk to an NFC reader directly. There is no need to have a SE in this case. Google Wallet was re-architected from a SIM-based SE to an HCE model to remove dependency on telecom operators. HCE was incorporated into the Android 4.4 operation system to support NFC secure transactions which include payments, loyalty programs, card access, and transit passes.

Security against authorized account access in HCE depends on four key concepts: limited use keys, tokenization, device fingerprinting, and dynamic risk analysis as follows:

- Limited use keys (LUK) are derived from a master domain key shared by the issuer and the cloud card management vendor.
- Tokenization reduces risk for banks by replacing the Personal Account Numbers (PAN) with a tokenized pseudo-PAN used in the payment system.
- Device profiles or "fingerprints" are intended to ensure transactions are initiated only by authorized user devices.
- User, device and account data is used to perform risk assessment for the transaction in real time (Roy, What is Hosted Card Emulation, 2014)

SE vs. HCE approach

- SE approach: in NFC card emulation mode, the card to be emulated is provisioned into a SE on the device through an app. When the user holds the device over an NFC reader, the NFC controller in the device routes data from the reader to the SE where the credential is saved for authentication (Figure 23).

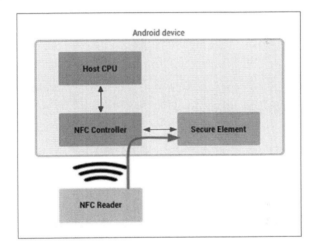

Figure 23: NFC card emulation with a secure element
Source: developer.android.com

- HCE approach: when the user holds the device over an NFC reader, the NFC controller in the device routes data from the reader to the host CPU on which applications are running (Figure 24).

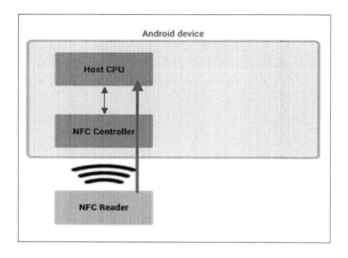

Figure 24: NFC card emulation without a SIM-based SE
Source: develop.google.com

The Impact of HCE Adoption

HCE simplified implementation is being adopted in various NFC secure applications including banking. The impact of HCE adoption is as follows:

- Investment on existing SE infrastructure: Some telecoms have made significant investment in order to build the infrastructure that utilizes the SIM-based SE. HCE is a threat to the return on such investments unless the existing infrastructure can be repurposed.

- TSM vendors: The TSM industry makes revenue by managing SE. The deployment of HCE eliminates the needs of SE. Therefore, the importance of MNO TSM diminishes. TSM vendors are seeking a new value proposition that attracts the market.

- The TEE solution: The TEE solution provides extra security for SE. Wide adoption of HCE will create a technology evolution for TEE in order to provide a stronger value proposition.

- The cost efficiency of HCE allows for more secure application development. It helps increasing NFC adoption.

Standards Groups' Position on HCE

On March 2014, NFC Forum confirmed that the use of HCE does not conflict with its own standards. It did, however recommend that, "service providers need to evaluate and determine the best place to store credentials for their solutions, keeping in mind the trade-off between security risks and convenience." (NFCForum, 2014).

SIMalliance published a whitepaper in April 14, 2014, entitled "Secure Element Deployment & Host Card Emulation v1.0". It stated that, "SIMallliance contends that while HCE is good for the NFC ecosystem as a whole, the technology remains immature, unstandardized, and relative to SE-based deployment, vulnerable to malicious attack." (simalliance, 2014)

NFC Mobile Wallet Summary

- Apple Pay: Tokens (Device Account Number) are generated based on EMVCo tokenization specification and stored in the embedded SE to identify credit cards. Actual credit card data is not stored in the SE or Apple's server.

- Softcard: EMV chip and PIN is used for tokenization. For each transaction, a different token is used. SIM-based SE is used to store credit card information that is downloaded "over the air" through a MNO TSM.

- Google Mobile Wallet: Authentication tokens are generated in the "Cloud" and pushed to the handset. For every transaction, a different token is used (Mick, 2014). HCE is used instead of SE.

Chapter 4: Who are the NFC Players?

Introduction

The NFC Ecosystem has been growing in the past few years. The unique combination of mobile and NFC technology has expanded the ecosystem.

Ecosystem players include manufacturers that produce mobile devices, smart cards, semiconductors, tags, readers and consumer electronics. Other ecosystem players are service providers including telecom operators, financial institutions, system integrators, certification organizations, merchants, marketing vendors, the printing and publishing industry and app developers.

Asia and Europe were early adopters of NFC technology. Various businesses have already started to use the technology to improve their outreach, processing time, mobile payments and customer service. For example, Singapore placed NFC terminals at over 20,000 places to accept mobile payments for purchases in 2012 (Khoo, 2012). Another example is McDonald's Happy Table. Daniel Lee, the director of Digital Projects at McDonald's, announced on August 22nd 2013, the rollout of the Happy Table in Asia at the MMA conference. The Happy Table is an initiative that transforms kids' tables in participating McDonald's into a play space utilizing NFC stickers. When an NFC-enabled phone or tablet is placed on the table, children are able to gain access to games and other activities via the NFC stickers underneath the table. (Low, 2013).

In Europe, Orange has launched its NFC Business Service Center to support companies in developing and deploying NFC secured services to customers of all the French mobile network operators. In London, NFC becomes part of the shopping experience in the Westfield London shopping Centre via digital pods supplied by CBS Outdoor UK. Germany's Volkwagen Bank is conducting an NFC payment pilot using iPhone4, 4S and 5 smartphones equipped with an iCate add-on case.

How can NFC technology be adopted in the US at a faster rate? Copperberg, a leader in event organizing, proposes that the ecosystem needs to unite in order to raise public awareness about the technology and show that it is not limited to another mobile payment solution (Mathis, 2013). One way to accomplish this is through the use of standard groups.

Standard Groups

When a new technology emerges, stakeholders often join efforts to form standards groups to advance the technology and minimize proprietary implementation. Currently, there are standards groups working on general NFC technology, as well as standards group working on NFC devices. The standards landscape interactive PowerPoint presentation is a good tool to understand the standards used in different NFC products and services.

The following standard groups are significant players in the NFC ecosystem. A brief description of the groups and their contributions towards the NFC standards are as follows:

NFC Forum

NFC Forum was established in 2004 and leads the effort for the unification of the NFC ecosystem. More than 180 companies are members of the NFC Forum. They share their expertise to develop the specifications and provide approval and certification for products. More than 20 specifications have been released (Figure 25). For more details about the specifications, please visit NFC Forum website at http://www.nfc-forum.org.

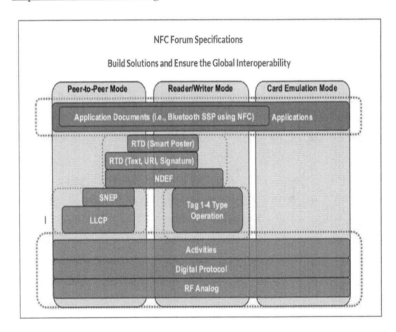

Figure 25: NFC Forum Specification Architecture

Source: NFC Forum goo.gl/IuUEmc

NFC Forum also established a brand mark "N-Mark" (Figure 26) to address stakeholder needs across the NFC ecosystem. NFC Forum recommends to use N-Mark as the universal symbol and touch point for NFC. It shows consumers where to touch their NFC-enabled device to initiate NFC actions. The guidelines for proper usage of N-Mark are provided at http://nfc-forum.org/our-work/nfc-branding/n-mark/

Figure 26: N-Mark

Smart Card Alliance

Formed in 2001, the Smart Card Alliance is a multi-industry association working to promote the understanding, adoption, use and widespread application of smart card technology (Vanderhoof, 2013). It has over 200 members. See more details at http://www.smartcardalliance.org

Global Platform

Launched in 1999, Global Platform has over 130 members. It standardizes the management of applications that are on the secure chip. It defines specifications for cards, devices and systems, as well as streamlines security requirements and testing through security certifications. It also confirms that a product's functionality aligns to the Global Platform technology through its Compliance Program. It addresses Secure Element (SE), Trusted Execution Environment (TEE) and Messaging. See more details at http://globalplatform.org

SIMAlliance

SIMalliance, founded in 2000, is the global, non-profit industry association which simplifies secure element (SE) implementation to drive the creation, deployment and management of secure mobile services. See more details at www.simaliance.org

The World Wide Web Consortium (W3C)

W3C, founded in 1994, is the main international standards organization for the World Wide Web standards. It defines an Open Web platform for application development that has the unprecedented potential to enable developers to build rich interactive experiences, powered by vast data stores that are available on any device. It published its first working draft on Web NFC API on January 14, 2014. See more details at www.w3.org/TR/nfc.

NFC Device Standards

Many groups are involved in the standardization of NFC-enabled devices. These efforts include integrating NFC technology into mobile devices, making sure that NFC transactions are secure and ensuring interoperability in the design of architecture.

- **GSM Association (GSMA)**

  Formed in 1995, the GSMA is an association of mobile operators and related companies devoted to supporting the standardization, deployment and promotion of the GSM mobile telephone system. See http://www.gsma.com/.

- **International Organization for Standardization /International Electrotechnical Commission (ISO/IEC)**

  Founded in 1947, the ISO/IEC publishes International Standards covering almost all aspects of technology and business.

  For NFC standards, ISO/IEC focuses on the card emulation interfaces. See http://www.iso.org.

- **European Computer Manufacturers Association (ECMA) International**

  Founded in 1961, ECMA is dedicated to the standardization of Information and Communication Technology (ICT) and Consumer Electronics (CE). (ECMAWeb, n.d.)

ECMA focuses on the interface between an NFC transceiver and a contactless front end (CLS). It works closely with ISO/IEC. See http://www.ecma-international.org/.

- **The European Telecommunications Standards Institute (ETSI)**

  Created in 1988, ETSI produces standards for Information and Communications Technologies (ICT), including fixed, mobile, radio, converged, broadcast and internet technologies (ETSIWeb, n.d.).

  ETSI focuses on interface between NFC APIs and the NFC controller. See http://www.etsi.org.

- **Java Community Process (JCP)**

  Introduced in 1998, JCP is the open, participative process to develop and revise the Java technology specifications, reference implementations and test suites (JCPWeb, n.d.).

  It focuses on JSR 257 and 177. See http://jcp.org.

- **Open Mobile Alliance (OMA)**

  Formed in June 2002, OMA delivers open specification for creating interoperable services that work across all geographical boundaries (OMAWeb, n.d.).

OMA focuses on browser and SCWS in the USIM for the UMTS network. See http://www.oenmobilealliance.org.

- **3rd Generation Partnership Project (3GPP)**

  Formed in 1998, 3GPP provides a stable environment to six telecommunications standard development organizations (ARIB, ATIS, CCSA, ETSI, TTA, TTC) in order to produce specifications that define 3GPP technologies (3GPPWeb, n.d.).

  3GPP focuses on NFC modem standardization. See http://www.3gpp.org.

- **Europay, MasterCard, Visa Cooperation (EMVCo)**

  Formed in 1993, EMVCo is a global standard for credit and debit payment cards based on chip card technology. EMVCo chip based payment cards are smart cards that contain an embedded microprocessor that has information needed for payment. (EMVWeb, n.d.)

  For NFC devices, EMVCo focuses on apps in the USIM (UMTS network). In March 2014, the EMVCo published Payment Tokenization Specification (EMVCo, 2014) sets the framework for tokenizing contactless payment. See http://www.emvco.com.

Chapter 5: Why Use NFC?

Introduction

"NFC creates a world of secure universal commerce and connectivity in which consumers can access and pay for physical or digital services, anywhere at any time with any devices." This was the vision shared by the NFC Forum at the Wireless CTIA in 2009, and it still rings true for technology visionaries across the globe.

ABI Research supported this vision when it reported that, "NFC is not just in mobile phones, tablets, PCs and peripherals, speaker docks, televisions, cameras, gaming and domestic appliances are all increasingly incorporating NFC" (ABI Research, NFC Installed Base, 2013).

Utilizing NFC can add the following values to your business:

- **Simplicity**: NFC simplifies data capture and expedites information collection, transfer and distribution. Unlike other connected technology, NFC doesn't require an app to exchange data or download information.
- **Accessibility**: NFC enables consumers to access content and services with a tap. This provides convenience for the consumers, especially those of the Y generation that are very connected to their mobile phones.
- **Security**: SIM card-based NFC provides ultimate security for mobile payment or non-payment secure applications such as transit or building access.

- **Cost efficiency**: NFC SIM cards and tags are relatively inexpensive compared to other currently utilized enablers.
- **Versatility**: NFC brings value to other electronics and creates new business opportunities.
- **Energy efficiency**: The passive nature of NFC chips doesn't require power resource.

Technology Overview on RFID, QR Code and Bluetooth

When people start understanding NFC technology, they often want to know what the differences are among NFC, QR Code and Bluetooth. Since NFC is based on RFID, questions are also asked about the differences between NFC and RFID. This section reviews these wireless connectivity technologies for curious minds.

NFC vs. RFID

NFC is based on RFID technology. RFID stands for Radio Frequency Identification. It is a small electronic device that consists of a chip and an antenna.

Here are some key points of contrast between NFC and RFID:

- NFC
  - Limited range of communication (4 centimeters)
  - Two-way communication
  - Three operating modes which enable a wide range of applications

- RFID
  - Tags are either active or passive. Active RFID tags can broadcast with a read range of up to 100 meters. Passive RFID tags have a read range of up to 25 meters (RFIDInsider, 2013).
  - One way communication: i.e. a reader detects and pulls information from a tag.
  - When more than one reader overlaps, an RFID tag is unable to respond to simultaneous queries. This is called Reader Collision.
  - When many tags are displayed in a small area, readers will be confused by all these signals. This is called Tag Collision.

NFC vs. QR code

A QR code (See Figure 27) is a two dimensional bar code that can store information. QR stands for Quick Response. It was invented in 1994 in Japan for the automotive industry and started to gain market share when its adoption rate began rising.

Figure 27: QR code

ScanLife released a survey entitled "Mobile Barcode Trend Report 2013 Q3" (Figure 28) which revealed some interesting statistics:

- Scanning activity is dramatically on the rise, now surpassing 180 scans per minute.
- There has been a 77% increase in new users.
- Android OS is responsible for 64% of QR code scans while iOS is responsible for 34%.

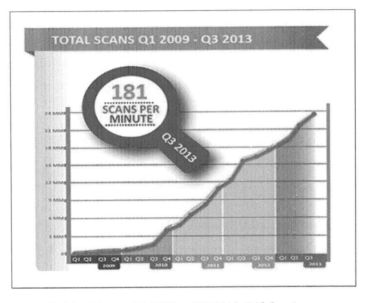

Figure 28: Total Scans Q1 2009 – Q3 2013 (LifeScan)

Q1 2014 survey showed that Mobile engagement is rapidly increasing, totally at 21.8 million scans this quarter. This activity is a 20 % increase from last year. iOS scan is up 46% from last year.

Here are some key points of contrast between NFC and QR codes:

- NFC
  - Needs NFC-enabled devices but does not require applications to use.
  - Not based on images scanned, but rather embedded tags that do not require visual cues to be detected by a device.
  - Tags are better for branding since they can be printed with color.
  - Tags are rewritable.
  - Tags have a secure mode option.
  - Communication mode is active to active or active to passive.

- QR code
  - Can be read by all smartphones with the proper applications.
  - Costs less than NFC.
  - Have market recognition.
  - Communication mode is passive; waiting for readers to scan.

NFC vs. Bluetooth

Bluetooth and NFC are both wireless connectivity technologies that communicate between devices over short distances.

Bluetooth was invented by Ericsson in 1994. It can connect 8 devices simultaneously and overcome problems of synchronization. When Bluetooth-capable devices come within range of one another, an electronic communication takes place to determine whether they have data to share, or whether one needs to control the other. Once the communication is complete, the devices form a network (Layton).

The differences between NFC and Bluetooth are as follows:

- NFC
    - Slower transfer speed (424 kbit/s)
    - Frequency 13.56 MHz
    - Communication mode is active to active or active to passive
    - Shorter range of connectivity (within 4 centimeters)
    - NFC's passive devices do not consume power
    - Works with passive devices

- Bluetooth
    - Faster speed (721 kbit/s)
    - Frequency 2.4 GHz
    - Longer range of connectivity (32 feet)
    - Communication mode is active to active
    - Conventional Bluetooth consumes more power, although the newer Bluetooth low energy (BLE) consumes less power than NFC
    - Does not work with passive devices
    - Requires devices to be paired by manual setup prior to communication
    - Data transfer is highly encrypted

BLE and Beacons

Bluetooth Low Energy (BLE)/Bluetooth Smart was originally introduced in 2006. It was merged into the main Bluetooth standard in 2010 with the adoption of the Bluetooth Core Specification Version 4.0.

BLE features:

- Ultra-low peak, average and idle mode power consumption
- Ability to run for years on standard coin-cell batteries
- Low cost
- Multi-vendor interoperability
- Enhanced range

Since it was adopted by iPhone 5 (iOS7) in September 2013, there have been many discussions over the benefits and drawbacks of NFC vs. BLE.

BLE-enabled devices listen for signals from Beacons (wireless transmitters). Since a BLE signal is always broadcasting, it can create one-to-many transmission relationships, in contrast to the one-to-one transmission relationships created by NFC.

With BLE transmission, a data packet is received by a device, a beacon ID is extracted from the packet by the OS, and the ID is made available to the appropriate app. The app then interrogates the ID to determine the next action (Stemle, 2014).

Summary and Looking Ahead

Summary

This book provides an overview of NFC technology by answering the following frequently asked questions:

- What is NFC
- Where is NFC Now
- How to use NFC
- Who are the NFC Players
- Why Use NFC

You now have a basic understanding of NFC technology. Your awareness will create a ripple effect that helps with the adoption of NFC technology.

The slow adoption rate that limits the growth of NFC technology is due to two issues. One is the lack of general NFC awareness. The second is that Apple does not offer the technology and it serves more than 40% of the Smartphone market (Siegal, 2014).

Lack of NFC general awareness:

Some consumers who have NFC-enabled phones don't know how to use them. Samsung has attempted to address this issue through its Galaxy commercial ads; however, more work in the area of education needs to occur in order to increase user awareness.

This point became evident in the case of Softcard Mobile

Wallet, where the raised awareness impacted the adoption rate. Softcard was rolled out nationwide in November 2013. It partnered with Jamba Juice for a campaign of one million free drinks that could be redeemed by Softcard users. Six months after launch on May 14, 2014; Softcard said consumers activated an average of 20,000 mobile wallets per day over the course of 30 days, doubling its growth rate from prior months. (http://paybefore.com, 2014)

Slow adoption of NFC by Apple:

While Apple was busy filing and receiving NFC patents, the NFC ecosystem was anxiously waiting for Apple to adopt NFC. In 2013, not only did Apple not adopt the NFC technology but it embraced BLE with iPhone 5s/5c release. BLE has been falsely framed as a competing technology to NFC. The following statistic shows the impact that Apple could have made if it had adopted NFC. In 2013, 275 million NFC devices were shipped and global iPhone sales was 150.26 million (Statista, 2014); more than ½ of NFC devices shipped.

Retailers and other solution providers were hesitant to go into the marketplace until they could reach the high percentage of smartphone users (Hunter, 2014). Apple finally provides an NFC solution for its mobile wallet with the release of Apple Pay for iPhone6/6+ in October, 2014. However, other than Apple Pay, all other NFC functionalities have not been activated for iPhone6 and iPhone 6+.

Looking Ahead

Since consumers are depending more on their mobile devices for a variety of services, mobile security is becoming a central concern. The fact that NFC could store sensitive information in a Secure Element is very appealing to consumers. Tapping creates a better user experience for the consumer and the ability to explore various mobile activities.

For businesses, NFC solutions bring a wealth of information about consumer buying habits, product and service consumption rates and the effectiveness of marketing campaigns. NFC moves big data into a new era. Through big data analytics, data initiated by or collected from NFC technology becomes meaningful and insightful. It provides retailers and manufacturers with the information that may improve their products or services.

From 2013 to 2014, new NFC products are being introduced at a more rapid pace with the increasing availability of NFC enabled devices, standardizations and technology awareness. Innovators also started to use P2P mode to create a better mobile wallet experience. For example, in 2015, Fortress payments will be launching a technology using P2P mode to make the mobile payment process transparent and intuitive for the consumer.

Given the complementary nature of BLE and NFC technology and Apple's inclusion of NFC in its Apple Pay, we can anticipate a quickening of widespread adoption from Apple users in the near future. Businesses that are ready to deploy the technology will benefit from it the most.

When it comes to iOS apps, it might take some time for Apple to build a software framework for developers. Until this framework is released, keeping NFC and its potential in the consciousness of consumers will rely on the ease of tapping to pay through the Apple Pay mobile payment. I expect when a software framework is offered, NFC open modes will be enabled by Apple and the iPhone6 will become a truly NFC enabled device. That will really help promoting NFC technology.

For secure transactions, the difference between the unstandardized implementation of TSM, HCE and SE might initially bring segmentation to the NFC ecosystem. However, the customer demand for universal purchasing services, painless account management and seamless integration with everyday activities will drive standardization. Increased collaboration in the NFC ecosystem will expedite this process.

The adoption of HCE will lead to a broader use of NFC and a less secure mobile payment. How TSM vendors and TEE solutions modify their business model and offers in order to meet the current need is critical. Francisco Corella, the CTO of Pomcor suggested that TEE provides virtual tamper resistance. The features physical tamper resistance either by itself or in conjunction with an SE (Francisco Corella, 2014). I think this type of innovation could provide TEE with a stronger value proposition.

I am envisioning a world that NFC is in our everyday lives. More products and services will come to the market when consumers and businesses see the value of using the technology. Consumers will become familiar with tapping in order to retrieve information and exchange data; as well as making an appointment, paying bills, monitoring health, transit use and building access.

Hopefully this book has sparked your imagination about the

possibilities of NFC in your businesses and lives. Be a technology pioneer and take advantage of the potential of this growing field. Thank you for reading.

Glossary

Acronym	Definition
API	Application Programming Interface
APP	Application
ARIB	Association of Radio Industries and Businesses, Japan
ATIS	Alliance for Telecommunications Industry Solutions, USA
BLE	Bluetooth Low Energy
CAGR	Compound Annual Growth Rate
CCSA	China Communications Standards Association
CLF	Contactless Frontend
Contact Smart Card	Require contact to initiate a transaction
DSLR	Digital single-lens reflex cameras
ECMA	European Computer Manufacturers Association
EMV	Europay, MasterCard and Visa

Acronym	Definition
EMVCo	Europay, MasterCard, Visa Cooperation
ETSI	European Telecommunications Standards Institute
iOS	iPhone OS (Operating System)
G&D	Giesecke & Devrient
GSMA	Global System for Mobile Communications Association
HDMI	High-Definition Multimedia Interface
IC	Integrated Circuit
JCP	Java Community Process
ISO/IEC	International Organization for Standardization/ International Electrotechnical Commission
LLCP	Logical Link Control Protocol (LLCP)
MNO	Mobile Network Operator
MWC	Mobile World Congress

Acronym	Definition
NDEF	NFC Data Exchange Format
NFC	Near Field Communication
OMA	Open Mobile Alliance
ORCA	One Region Card for All
OTA	Over the Air
POS	Point of Sale
QR	Quick Response
RTD	Record Type Definition
RFID	Radio Frequency Identification
SCWS	Smart Card Web Server
SE	Secure Element
SIM	Subscriber Identification Module
SNEP	Simple NDEF Exchange Protocol
SP	Service Provider
TEE	Trusted Execution Environment
TSM	Trust Service

Acronym	Definition
TTA	Telecommunications Technology Association, Korea
TTC	Telecommunication Technology Committee, Japan
UICC	Universal Integrated Circuit Card
UMTS	The Universal Mobile Telecommunications System
USIM	The SIM application for UMTS network
URI	Unified Resource Identifier
USIM	Universal Identity Subscriber Module
USB	Universal Serial Bus
W3C	The World Wide Web Consortium
WIFI	Is a technology that allows an electronic device to exchange data or connect to the internet wirelessly using radio waves

Acronym	Definition
Y Generation	There are no precise dates for when Y Generation starts and ends. Commentators use beginning birth dates from the early 1980 to the early 2000s.

Works Cited

3GPPWeb. (n.d.). *About 3GPP*. Retrieved 9 14, 2013, from
http://www.3gpp.org: http://www.3gpp.org/About-
3GPP

ABI Research. (2012, 11 2). *NFC will Come Out of the Trial Phase*.
Retrieved from ABIresearch:
http://www.abiresearch.com/press/nfc-will-come-
out-of-the-trial-phase-in-2013-as-28

ABI Research. (2013, 3 26). *NFC Installed Base*. Retrieved from
ABI Research:
https://www.abiresearch.com/press/nfc-installed-
base-to-exceed-500m-devices-within-1

ABLOY, A. (2013, March 4th). *Seos : Powering Mobile Access*.
Retrieved from ASSA ABLOY:
http://www.assaabloy.com/en/com/Press-
News/News/2013/Seos-rides-NFC-wave-at-Mobile-
World-Congress/

Admin, N. (2011, dec 28). *Development with Android Beam and
NFC Peer-2-Peer*. Retrieved from www.nfc.cc:
http://www.nfc.cc/2011/12/28/development-
android-beam-and-nfc-peer-2-peer/

Allprnews. (2013, 8 13). *Near Field Communication Applications
Market* . Retrieved from http://allprnews.com/:
http://allprnews.com/near-field-communication-
applications-market-to-reach-10015-96-million-by-

2016-at-a-cagr-of-38-from-2011-to-2016-new-report-
by-marketsandmarkets

Apple. (2014, 9 12). *Apple Pay*. Retrieved from www.apple.com:
http://www.apple.com/iphone-6/apple-pay/

Balaban, D. (2013, 7 31). *Qualcomm to Integrate Trusted Execution
Environment with NFC Technology*. Retrieved from NFC
Times: http://nfctimes.com/news/qualcomm-
integrate-tee-nfc-technology

BluetoothSIG. (2014). *Bluetooth Smart (Low Energy)*. Retrieved
from Bluetooth Developer Portal:
https://developer.bluetooth.org/TechnologyOvervie
w/Pages/BLE.aspx

Boden, R. (2013, 8 13). *NFC World*. Retrieved from Coca-Cola
runs NFC promotion in 100 stores:
http://www.nfcworld.com/2013/08/13/325454/coca
-cola-runs-nfc-promotion-in-stores/

Boden, R. (2014, 6 11). *Nintendo unveils Amiibo NFC figures that
work with multiple Wii U and 3DS games*. Retrieved from
MFC World:
http://www.nfcworld.com/2014/06/11/329632/nint
endo-unveils-amiibo-nfc-figures-work-multiple-wii-u-
3ds-games/

Boden, R. (2014, 6 19). *Tap2Tag launches NFC medical alert
devices*. Retrieved from http://www.nfcworld.com:
http://www.nfcworld.com/2014/06/19/329805/tap2
tag-launches-nfc-medical-alert-devices/

Buckley, S. (2013, 9 5). *Verizon Wireless shows off NFC wares*

during the NY State Fair. Retrieved from
www.fiercetelecom.com:
http://www.fiercetelecom.com/story/verizon-
wireless-shows-nfc-wares-during-ny-state-fair/2013-
09-05

BusinessWire. (2013, 7 30). *Isis® Announces National Rollout
Later This Year* . Retrieved from
www.businesswire.com:
http://www.businesswire.com/news/home/20130730
006909/en/Isis%C2%AE-Announces-National-
Rollout-Year

BusinessWire. (2014, 8 22). *Nanjing Youth Olympic Village
Promotes High-Tech Socializing.* Retrieved from Business
Wire:
http://www.businesswire.com/news/home/20140822
005137/en/Nanjing-Youth-Olympic-Village-
Promotes-High-Tech-Socializing#%2EU_xig7y1Yc8

Cattaneo, P. (2014). TEE Conference . *Global Platform Second
Annaul Conference* (pp. Identity, authentication &
Payments Panel). Santa Clara: Global Platform.

Chang, H.-h. (2013, 9 7). *Apple and NFC.* Retrieved from
EverydayNFC:
http://everydaynfc.com/2013/09/07/apple-and-nfc/

Clark, S. (2011, 5 31). *RIM releases BlackBerry NFC APIs.*
Retrieved from NFC World:
http://www.nfcworld.com/2011/05/31/37778/rim-
releases-blackberry-nfc-apis/

Clark, S. (2013, June 12). *ABI reports NFC chip market shares.* Retrieved from NFO World: http://www.nfcworld.com/2013/06/12/324581/abi-reports-nfc-chip-market-shares/

Clark, S. (2013, 8 13). *TapCheck to launch NFC medical devices.* Retrieved from NFC World: http://www.nfcworld.com/2013/08/13/325472/tapc heck-to-launch-nfc-medical-devices/

Clark0925, S. (2012, 9 25). *Inside Secure to offer cloud-based NFC secure element solution.* Retrieved from http://www.nfcworld.com/: http://www.nfcworld.com/2012/09/25/318059/insi de-secure-to-offer-cloud-based-nfc-secure-element-solution/

Davies, J. (2012, 4 11). *Hands on: The Lumia 610, Nokia's first Windows NFC phone.* Retrieved from NFC World: http://www.nfcworld.com/2012/04/11/315025/han ds-on-the-lumia-610-nokias-first-windows-nfc-phone/

ECMAWeb. (n.d.). *What is ECMA.* Retrieved 9 14, 2013, from http://www.ecma-international.org: http://www.ecma-international.org/memento/index.html

EMVCo. (2014, 3). *Payment Tokenisation.* Retrieved from www.emvco.com: http://www.emvco.com/specifications.aspx?id=263

EMVWeb. (n.d.). *About EMV.* Retrieved 9 13, 2013, from https://www.emvco.com/: https://www.emvco.com/

ETSIWeb. (n.d.). *About ETSI*. Retrieved 9 14, 2013, from
    http://www.etsi.org: http://www.etsi.org/about

Forums, N. (2006, 7 24). The NFC Data Exchang Format
    technical specification.

Francisco Corella, P. (2014, 9 25). *Smart Cards, TEEs and
    Derived Credentials*. Retrieved from Promcor:
    http://pomcor.com/2014/09/25/smart-cards-tees-
    and-derived-credentials/

Gillick, K. (n.d.). *GlobalPlatform made simple guide: Trusted
    Execution Environment (TEE) Guide*. Retrieved 9 12,
    2013, from http://www.globalplatform.org:
    http://www.globalplatform.org/mediaguidetee.asp

Global Platform. (2013, 2 27). *GlobalPlatform Specification
    Supports Service Provider Integration into the NFC Ecosystem*.
    Retrieved from http://www.globalplatform.org/:
    http://www.globalplatform.org/mediapressview.asp?i
    d=982

Heisler, Y. (2014, 10 2). *Apple Pay: An in-depth look at what's
    behind the secure payment system*. Retrieved from
    www.tuaw.com:
    http://www.tuaw.com/2014/10/02/apple-pay-an-in-
    depth-look-at-whats-behind-the-secure-payment/

http://paybefore.com. (2014, May 15th).
    http://paybefore.com/pay-news. Retrieved from
    http://paybefore.com: http://paybefore.com/pay-
    news/isis-touts-600000-monthly-account-activations-
    as-pace-doubles-may-15-2014/

http://www.fastcasual.com. (2014, 7 23). *http://www.fastcasual.com/news*. Retrieved from http://www.fastcasual.com/news/jamba-juice-gives-away-millionth-beverage-to-isis-mobile-wallet-user/: http://www.fastcasual.com/news/jamba-juice-gives-away-millionth-beverage-to-isis-mobile-wallet-user/

Hunter, P. (2014, 9 10). *NFC Forum*. Retrieved from www.nfc-forum.org: http://nfc-forum.org/newsroom/analysts-apple-pay-will-help-spur-wider-usage-of-mobile-payments/

IHS. (2014, 2 27). *NFC-Enabled Cellphone Shipments to Soar Fourfold in Next Five Years* . Retrieved from http://press.ihs.com: http://press.ihs.com/press-release/design-supply-chain/nfc-enabled-cellphone-shipments-soar-fourfold-next-five-years

JCPWeb. (n.d.). *FAQ*. Retrieved 9 14, 2013, from http://jcp.org: http://jcp.org/en/introduction/faq#speclead

Khoo, N. A. (2012, 8 23). *You can finally use NFC for payments in Singapore*. Retrieved from Cnet: http://asia.cnet.com/you-can-finally-use-nfc-for-payments-in-singapore-62218405.htm

King County. (n.d.). *Fares & ORCA*. Retrieved 9 11, 2013, from http://metro.kingcounty.gov: http://metro.kingcounty.gov/fares/orca/index.html

Layton, C. F. (n.d.). *How Bluetooth Works*. Retrieved from Howstuffworks: http://electronics.howstuffworks.com/bluetooth.htm

Low, A. (2013, 8 22). *McDonald's NFC Happy Table will be rolling out to rest of Asia.* Retrieved from CNET/Asia: http://asia.cnet.com/mcdonalds-nfc-happy-table-will-be-rolling-out-to-rest-of-asia-62222156.htm?src=twt

MacDailyNews. (2013, 1 22). *Apple iPhone continues lead with 51.2% U.S. market share as Android users increasingly switch to iPhone.* Retrieved from http://macdailynews.com: http://macdailynews.com/2013/01/22/apple-iphone-continues-lead-with-51-2-u-s-market-share-as-android-users-increasingly-switch-to-iphone/

MarketsandMarkets. (2014, 7 31). *Near field communication market worth $16.25 billion by 2022.* Retrieved from http://www.whatech.com/: http://www.whatech.com/market-research-reports/press-release/telecommunications/26025-near-field-communication-market-worth-16-25-billion-by-2022

Mathis, R. (2013, 7 22). *Survey: Why NFC has not fully taken off yet.* Retrieved from SecureIDNews: http://secureidnews.com/news-item/survey-why-nfc-has-not-fully-taken-off-yet/

McGregor, J. (2013, 8 31). *How high-fiving your front door can let you can ditch the keys.* Retrieved from www.techradar.com: http://www.techradar.com/news/world-of-tech/future-tech/how-high-fiving-your-front-door-can-let-you-can-ditch-the-keys-1175279

Mick, J. (2014, 9 8). *Apple's Lagging Adoption of Token-Protected NFC Mistaken For "Innovation"*. Retrieved from DailyTech:
http://www.dailytech.com/Apples+Lagging+Adoptio n+of+TokenProtected+NFC+Mistaken+For+Innova tion/article36518.htm

News, N. (2010, 4 20). *Open NFC API for Android™ now available*. Retrieved from NXP:
http://www.nxp.com/news/press-releases/2010/04/open-nfc-api-for-android-now-available.html

Newswire, E. (2013, 12 23). *ABI Research - Smartphones Accounting for 4 out of 5 NFC Devices as 2013* . Retrieved from Hispanicbusiness.com:
http://www.hispanicbusiness.com/2013/12/23/abi_r esearch_-_smartphones_accounting_for.htm

NFC World. (2013, 6 5). *News in brief*. Retrieved from NFC World:
http://www.nfcworld.com/2013/06/05/324392/dell-adds-nfc-to-xps-12-laptop/

NFCForum. (2014, 3 20). *NFC Forum*. Retrieved from http://nfc-forum.org: http://nfc-forum.org/newsroom/nfc-forum-issues-statement-on-host-card-emulation/

NFC-Forum. (n.d.). *NFC Forum Technical Specifications*. Retrieved 9 15, 2013, from http://www.nfc-forum.org: http://www.nfc-forum.org/specs/spec_list/

OMAWeb. (n.d.). *About OMA.* Retrieved 9 14, 2013, from
http://openmobilealliance.org:
http://openmobilealliance.org/about-oma/

PhoneArena. (2012, 3 27). *30 million NFC phones were shipped in
2011, huge growth ahead.* Retrieved from
www.phonearena.com:
http://www.phonearena.com/news/30-million-NFC-
phones-were-shipped-in-2011-huge-growth-
ahead_id28470

Raschke, K. (2011, February 10). *FareBot: reading ORCA cards on
Android.* Retrieved from
http://transport.kurtraschke.com:
http://transport.kurtraschke.com/2011/02/farebot-
orca-android

RFIDInsider. (2013, 4 22). *RFID vs. NFC: What's the Difference?*
Retrieved from http://blog.atlasrfidstore.com/rfid-vs-
nfc: http://blog.atlasrfidstore.com/rfid-vs-
nfc#sthash.xqDnmqot.dpuf

Roy, K. (2014, 7 16). *What is Hosted Card Emulation.* Retrieved
from www.sequent.com:
http://www.sequent.com/host-card-emulation/

Roy, K. (2014). *What is tokenization.* Retrieved from
www.sequent.com: http://www.sequent.com/what-is-
tokenization/

ScanLife. (2013, 8 1). *Trend Report 2013 Q2.* Retrieved from
http://www.scanlife.com:
http://www.scanlife.com/trend-reports/q2-

2013/CAX346UGKSM

Siegal, J. (2014, 1 10). *Despite hot sales, iPhone 5s, 5c may not be winning fresh converts*. Retrieved from BGR: http://bgr.com/2014/01/10/apple-iphone-market-share-2013/

simalliance. (2014, 4 29). *simalliance*. Retrieved from http://www.simalliance.org/: http://www.simalliance.org/en/se/se_marketing/sec ure-element-deployment--host-card-emulation--v1_hs4nruef.html

Statista. (2014). *Global Apple iPhone Sales since fiscal year 2007*. Retrieved from The Statistics Portal: http://www.statista.com/statistics/276306/global-apple-iphone-sales-since-fiscal-year-2007/

Stemle, C. (2014, 1 31). *BLE vs. NFC: The future of mobile consumer engagement now [infographic]*. Retrieved from Mobile Payments Today: http://www.mobilepaymentstoday.com/blogs/ble-vs-nfc-the-future-of-mobile-consumer-engagement-now-infographic/

Vanderhoof, R. (2013). Mobile/NFC Security Fundamentals. *Smart Card Alliance and Global Platform Webinar.* http://www.smartcardalliance.org/resources/webinar s/Anatomy_of_a_Mobile_Device_030513.pdf. Retrieved from http://www.smartcardalliance.org/resources/webinar s/Anatomy_of_a_Mobile_Device_030513.pdf

Whitney, L. (2014, 9 16). *Subway to use Softcard NFC for mobile payments*. Retrieved from www.cnet.com: http://www.cnet.com/news/subway-restaurants-to-use-softcard-nfc-for-mobile-payments/

wiiudaily. (2014). *http://wiiudaily.com/wii-u-nfc/*. Retrieved from http://wiiudaily.com: http://wiiudaily.com/wii-u-nfc/

XDA. (2013, 8 20). *NFC tags*. Retrieved from XDA Developer Forum: http://forum.xda-developers.com/wiki/NFC_Tags